Love Is Not...
A Devotional and Drama Resource

by
Dana McAfee

DORRANCE PUBLISHING CO
EST. 1920
PITTSBURGH, PENNSYLVANIA 15238

The contents of this work, including, but not limited to, the accuracy of events, people, and places depicted; opinions expressed; permission to use previously published materials included; and any advice given or actions advocated are solely the responsibility of the author, who assumes all liability for said work and indemnifies the publisher against any claims stemming from publication of the work.
All Rights Reserved

Copyright © 2021 by Dana McAfee

No part of this book may be reproduced or transmitted, downloaded, distributed, reverse engineered, or stored in or introduced into any information storage and retrieval system, in any form or by any means, including photocopying and recording, whether electronic or mechanical, now known or hereinafter invented without permission in writing from the publisher.

Dorrance Publishing Co
585 Alpha Drive
Pittsburgh, PA 15238

Visit our website at www.dorrancebookstore.com

ISBN: 978-1-6495-7048-2
EISBN: 978-1-6491-3893-4

Dedicated to my mom, my biggest fan.
You are my example of unconditional love.

Acknowledgment

Thank you, Erin Leinbach for encouraging me to follow this dream. Dannielle Boggs-Robertson, you have urged me to follow excellence and taken time to invest in my life, thank you. Jim Cox, I love my cover!

Dana McAfee

I am tired… tired of anger, hatred, war, bullying, deceit, backstabbing, judgment, loneliness, fear. Love seems to be dying out and complacency is taking over. I am not without fault, but there needs to be a change.

1st Corinthians 13 says love is patient, kind, doesn't envy, doesn't boast, isn't proud, isn't rude, isn't self-seeking, not easily angered, keeps no record of wrongs, doesn't delight in evil, rejoices with the truth, protects, trusts, hopes, perseveres, and never fails. Quite a list of what seems to be impossible these days. It also says in I John 4:16 that God is love, so there seems to be an obvious solution. The world needs love and the world needs God.

So, where have we all gone wrong? What's the answer? How do we change? How do we overcome and do what seems to be impossible? I am beginning to explore these things as I look to an answer. I don't want to be tired; I want to be energized! In my search, I decided to focus on these principles and discover what love is not. We all want love; we feel empty without it, so let's try to make a difference in our own lives in order to make a difference in the lives of others.

#1
Love does not rush in

"Patience is the art of hoping" - *Luc De Clapiers*

If there is one thing that is running low in our society today it is patience. We want fast everything: internet, food, friendships, cars, love...connections. We just don't have time to waste. However, when we do finally rush into most of these things, we discover that they don't last:

- Food...we get hungry again, in the same day
- Internet...a new system comes along in a few months
- Friendships...we leave our current environment and move on
- Cars...wear, tear, rust, miles
- Love...we realize we don't know the person at all

We forgo true connections with people today because we don't take time to truly get to know them. We want the instant "magic," the fireworks, the passion/fire, the thrill. When it all comes down to it, magic is an illusion, fireworks fizzle, fire burns out leaving scars, and thrills are for amusement parks. We enjoy those things while they last, but the point is…they come to an end. We don't want love to come to an end, and it shouldn't. So, how do we build patience in such a fast-paced society, especially when something as important as love is at stake? We want to make good, smart, heartfelt decisions that will last a lifetime and not just in romantic relationships but also with family and friends.

We are born into our families, so most of us don't have a choice. We have years to build up the relationships and deal with the dysfunctions that happen at various levels. Patience is usually at the center of a family; patience is the heart. We argue, we disappoint each other, we deceive, we tease, but we want to love. No matter how many mistakes we make we have to patiently look at the situation and make a decision: Are we finished with that person or do we help each other change and grow? It isn't easy, I know. We won't always get it right and we will get tired of the same person making the same mistakes and bad choices over and over again. Patient love allows us to continue working on those relationships and the chance to show the love that God intended. We don't need to accept the choices or condone the behavior but, maybe, it will be there when they hit rock bottom and need a hand to help them climb out.

Love is Not...

We do choose our friends, and they choose us. There are many growth spurts where friendships are concerned: childhood buddies, teen transitions, college connections (that often stay with us through adulthood), and adult confidants. At each stage of these relationships, each friend seems to be the most important person in life, but life moves on and we move in different directions. Patient love is what maintains the best friendships. My best friends today are those people who have shared experiences that connected us. We all have different lifestyles: married, single, kids, jobs, and hobbies. It takes much patience to make these friendships last through all of that! Rescheduling time to meet with their needs, weeks and months going by and not hearing from them, opposite vacation times but these are the friends with whom I have shared my fears, fantasies, joys, and defeats...I don't want to lose them. Patience is the key and "a friend loves at all times." (Prov. 17:17.)

Romance and patience do not go hand in hand these days. I might be at one end of the spectrum: one boyfriend in high school, no dates at all in college, one relationship outside of college, and married in my late twenties. Married almost six years and his patience wore out. He was ready to be married to someone else. Several years later (two marriages and divorces for him), we reconnected for about a

Dana McAfee

year. He drops out of the scene again. A couple of years later (you guessed it) we reconnect again and, this time, it is for three years and…wait for it…he pulls away again. I had loved him for almost twenty-five years and had been patiently waiting for him to want me again, but patient love does not require me to be used over and over again. I have finally learned that. Instead, patient love should grow in a twenty-five-year relationship, learning about each other and still being fascinated, understanding the differences and working on the shortcomings. It is wanting the very best for the other person for the rest of your lives. True love makes you a priority, doesn't have to struggle to love you, doesn't change its mind every few years. Imagine if God's love wasn't patient. Where would we be right now? He patiently waits for us to know Him, believe in Him, and love Him in return. He is waiting for that day when we will want that forever relationship with him. Wow!

Grace – twenty-three years old
Jim – twenty-five years old.

A young couple sitting at a nice restaurant looking at menus

Grace: Wow, this is such a nice place; are you sure you can afford this? It's quite a splurge.

Love is Not...

Jim: Anything for my girl on our six-month anniversary. I want tonight to be special.

Grace: That's really sweet, but you just started your new job and I'm finishing school. We need to be careful with spending. I graduate in a month. There is so much to do for both of us.

Jim: I'm glad you brought that up because there is an important question I want to ask you and I thought this place would be special.

Grace: Wait a second. Oh, Jim, I hope it isn't what I think you are going to ask. We really need to slow down a minute. I'm not sure you are thinking this through right now.

Jim: I don't need more time. I believe God put you in my life for a reason and know we'll be together forever. Why wait? We connected right from the beginning and I know we love each other.

Grace: I think this is a very special relationship too, but I don't feel the need to rush. Dating six months is just scratching the surface. If we really believe God has put us together, then that won't change in a year. It won't change in ten years.

Jim: But I'm so certain. I want to begin my life with you.

Grace: We have started. This is the beginning. We have plenty of time to build this relationship. You get settled into your new job and I will graduate and find a job and we can travel that road together.

Jim: (pause) I am always going full-steam ahead. Another reason I believe God put you in my life—common sense! We can also start saving and planning for the big stuff. I guess somewhere deep down I am afraid this will all end and I will lose you, which is silly if I really believe God has brought us together. (pause) Can we still have a nice dinner? This all looks amazing.

Grace: I guess we can splurge this time. (Takes his hand) I love you, Jim. Thanks for understanding… and you will not lose me.

Jim: You are worth listening to. This will be one great adventure. Waiter!

#2
Love is not Indifferent

"Be a rainbow in someone else's cloud" - Maya Angelou

I have been a high school teacher for twenty-nine years now. I love my job... I love the type of work; I love the students; I love that I get to know families. I hate the intimidation and bullying that can take place; it breaks my heart. According to the website, getsmarter.com, there are 2.1 million bullies in American schools, 2.7 victims of bullying K–12, and 1 in 7 students is either a bully or a victim of a bully. The disease of bullying infiltrates a life, eats away at a person's emotions and self-respect, and leaves scars. A possible cure for this disease? Kindness.

Think about all of the ways in your life you have been shown kindness, on any level: the person who sat with you at lunch, the friend who cried with you after a breakup, that group of friends who helped you move, that stranger who smiled at you on one of your worst days, the one who sat with you while a loved one was in surgery, the student who stepped in and stopped the bullying. There was no cost to any of these acts of kindness, but the impact it left was truly priceless.

We can sit and watch the news every night and see the devastation, brutality, and bad choices but there are also people in this world who practice random acts of kindness… We need more stories about these people! These simple acts can change a life forever. Some examples:

- Let the other car have your parking space
- Visit a nursing home and read to someone
- Shovel your neighbor's driveway
- Let someone go in front of you at the checkout
- Sit with a new kid at lunch
- Write an encouraging note to your teacher
- Do a chore for your sibling, or spouse

I could fill this page with more ideas, but you get the picture… kind things, random acts at no cost that encourage others.

Relationships today can use more kindness. It is usual that if you love someone, there is kindness that grows, but I also believe that love can grow out of kindness. It is so easy to let the everyday difficulties in life take charge of our attitudes. A bad day and we take it out on each other. Instead, we could

Love is Not...

counteract the negative with something kind. For every kind act you do, the capacity for love expands and your heart seems to grow a bit. Colossians 3:12 tells us to clothe ourselves with kindness, which implies completeness. We choose the clothes we wear every day. Why not choose kindness?

Tina – Young woman in her twenties.
Burst through the door, throws down her purse, and begins to pace. Eventually sits.

Tina: I thought I was finished with this in high school. "Little miss perfect," "aces every test" "thinks she's better than everyone." I just want to work hard and do my best; I really think that is what God wants from me. I got good grades in school because I wanted to. Teased about not dating, teased about not having the best clothes, teased about being quiet. College was a little better because we were all fairly focused on our own things and had a goal to achieve. Now that I've started a new job, I am getting the same junk thrown at me. "She's brown-nosing the boss," "she's not friendly," "she thinks she's smarter than us." Even my so-called friends are giving me a hard time. I know they think they are just teasing, but it brings back those bad memories. I don't want to change the personality God has given me, but I don't know how much more of this I can take. A little understanding and encouragement would be so nice for a change. Different, but nice. (stands and picks up purse) God wants my best so I will keep doing my best. Maybe, one day, others around me will understand. Until then Lord, give me the strength for tomorrow. (exits the room).

#3
Love does not envy

"Contentment is not the fulfillment of what you want, but the realization of how much you already have"
– Anonymous

It seems one of the biggest problems facing relationships today is the feeling that we might have missed something better. We experience this with other things like phones, computers, cars, houses, vacations. Proverbs 14:30 says, "A heart at peace gives life to the body but envy rots the bones." A relationship, however, involves another human being with emotions and insecurities, so we shouldn't be trying them out like a new car, hobby, or wardrobe.

Webster's Dictionary defines envy as "discontent because of the possessions or good fortune of another." We are attracted to someone, start a relationship, make a commitment and then start to look at what everyone else has: someone more attractive, a better a leader, a better lover, richer, nicer, a better listener. It could never end. We need to appreciate the love we have been given and realize that we may not be the end-all prize ourselves! Let's face it, every person on the planet has some flaw and imperfection. When we have the start of a new relationship, there is this magical spell that seems to occur where all of those flaws are invisible. We then seem to expect that perfection for happily ever after, and when the relationship progresses, the imperfections seem to pop up like weeds. Now there is a choice, do we embrace the things we love about that person or do we go in search of another who has the traits we used to find most interesting. The cycle begins again.

The best choice is to let go of the envy completely and dig deeper into the wonderful things about the person we have chosen, and who chose us. There is something genuine, sweet, attractive, and inspiring about someone who knows you completely and loves you in spite of all your complexities and dysfunctions. Why not turn your journey together into an adventure? Discover new things about each other, make fun memories, experience the first love. Make everyone else curious about what you have... just don't rub it in!

Brian – midthirties.
Enters through the door after a long day.

Brian: What a day! I can't believe I had to work today

Love is Not...

when all of the big-wigs got to go off on their yachts and sports cars, doing whatever they want. I'll never have a nice car, or house, or even go on a nice vacation. I work like crazy just to pay the bills and buy food and have nothing left over. I would give anything to trade places with one of them. I feel cheated. When am I going to get some of the good things? (Wife and kids walk through the door, wife kisses him, and they exit into the other room. He looks after them). Okay, maybe I wouldn't trade places. Not everyone has a job to go to, a house, or food, and certainly not everyone has an amazing family like mine! (He sits and bows his head). Forgive me, Lord. Teach me to appreciate the gifts you have given me. I am truly blessed. (He rises and goes off toward his family)

#4
Love is not boastful

*"It matters not what you are thought to be,
but what you are"*

– *Publilius Syrus*

There is nothing more annoying than a person walking around with their figurative megaphone shouting, for all to hear, about all of their accomplishments, position, wealth, etc. Everything they have and we don't. Boasting, applauding themselves, showing what good people they are. If they would only realize that truly accomplished people don't need to do any of that, their deeds would show for themselves. Sometimes it is just better to remain anonymous, since real love and self-respect don't need to prove anything; they just need to remain steadfast and pure. "…don't let your left hand know what your right hand is doing" Matthew 6:3.

Occasionally at school we have a time when the students are asked to write letters of encouragement to their teachers. Some of my most blessed memories are those little notes that were written especially for me. It is even more precious when

Dana McAfee

it comes from a student I would never have expected. I had no idea they felt that way or that they were learning anything from me. My cedar chest at home is filled with notes I have received over the last twenty-nine years, and when I am having a particularly hard time, or wonder why I became a teacher in the first place, I open that chest and read. I am quickly reminded.

I love to watch children who are trying to surprise a parent with a special treasure. They giggle and hide and wait for their parents to look away so they can place a trinket or picture they have drawn in a special place, to be found later. The parent then finds the treasure and they reply with something along the lines of, "My goodness, where did this come from?" or "I wonder who left this for me?" The children are pleased with their anonymous accomplishment. We all need to get back to that childlike innocence where a simple smile or a thankful tear is all we need.

Carl – Late forties, Dan – Midtwenties
Sitting in a coffee shop

Carl: I'm so glad we found time to get together. How have things been going?

Dan: Awesome! I feel like things couldn't be better and

Love is Not...

              I am in the best place I can be. I got that promotion at work, so now Sandy and I can take that big vacation we've always wanted. We are going this summer.

Carl: That's nice, I'm sure you will—

Dan: I figured it was about time. I work really hard, you know. I think we deserve it. I might even look into getting a new car, now that we can afford it.

Carl: Oh, did something happen to your car? I thought it was just a couple of years old.

Dan: No, it's fine. It would just be nice to have one that isn't used and has all of the bells and whistles.

Carl: That seems like a lot of money being spent pretty fast. What if something goes wrong?

Dan: What could go wrong? We both have good jobs and no kids yet. Why not splurge? You and Nancy are great examples.

Carl: We do have a great marriage and wonderful kids, but nothing is perfect all the time.

Dan: What are you talking about?

Carl: I got laid off Friday.

Dan: What? I thought your job was really secure?

Carl: Nothing is completely secure. I'm just glad I have saved up over the years. We will be fine for a while.

Dana McAfee

Dan: I am so sorry. I get way too wrapped up in myself sometimes. I need to step back a bit. Is there anything I can do for you guys?

Carl: Thanks, but we are really okay. I would like you to think about your future, though. Think sensibly; think with caution.

Brian: I just got so excited about the promotion and thinking of all the things I could do. I've worked hard and I want to make Sandy happy.

Carl: Has she mentioned that she is unhappy?

Brian: No, she's an angel and supports me in everything.

Carl: So, you really need to think about supporting her too, especially for your future.

Brian: I never thought about it that way. I know my car is definitely fine for now and we could certainly scale down our vacation quite a bit. I could take the extra money from the promotion and put it into savings. I would, however, love to meet with you occasionally to work out a budget, if you wouldn't mind. Not my strong suit.

Carl: Not at all! It would be my pleasure. (They get up to leave) I'll talk to Nancy and call you tomorrow to set up a time. Maybe all four of us could meet together (They exit).

#5
Love is not proud

"Everyone needs a house to live in, but a supportive family is what builds a home"
– Anthony Liccione

I can be an extremely independent person and often think that I don't need anyone. I have been on my own almost half of my life. God has provided for all of my needs and has blessed me with an incredible, fulfilling job. I can take care of myself just fine, but that doesn't mean I always want it that way. I can let my pride get the best of me and then I miss out on some amazing collaborative experiences.

I am a high school theater teacher. I am in charge of making sure productions and programs go off without a hitch. When I first started teaching, I did most of it by myself. Sometimes I chose it that way and sometimes I didn't have much of a choice. The past ten years, I have discovered the beautiful art of collaboration and the importance of a support system. I have builders, designers, costumers, stage crew, technicians, Booster parents, and the list goes on. This has been incredibly

Dana McAfee

important for a sound mind, a restful spirit, and an amazing finished product! I look back at our productions the past ten years and am amazed at the beauty, quality, and love that has gone into each one. It is okay to take pride in a job well done, even Peter did when he was establishing his own ministry. (Romans 11:13) I am certainly proud of my students and the team I work with every year. I am blessed!

I have also been through a heartbreaking divorce that I never expected to have to deal with. Being, also, a psychology major in college, I figured I could handle the situation myself. I knew the principles, the jargon, the tools, and the end product that was expected. It never completely occurred to me how much I would need the support of my family, friends, and a professional counselor. Their love and support brought me through some of my darkest days. I was able to look at things from a different perspective, realize that it wasn't all my fault, and begin to heal. I know God gave me the strength to get out of bed every day, but the people He put in my life showed me how to move on and take care of myself. Once my pride was gone I could find healing through the people who were placed in my life for that very season. I am still afraid that I will never trust again because that limits my relationships, but I know I can love with God's love and not be afraid because … "perfect love casts out fear." (1 John 4:18)

Love is Not...

We also have the consistent support of a God whose love never fades. We have a hard time connecting to that because people leave us, disappoint us, and hurt us. He left any appearance of pride in heaven, came to earth, lived among us, succumbed to torture, died on a cross, and rose from the dead so that we would never have to be without support again. We need to be that kind of support to others when they can't, or won't, see him. Sometimes in the background, sometimes lifting them up, walking with them through the struggles, loving them in the simple ways.

Kim and Lisa – Two young mothers
Sitting on a couch in a living room

Kim: I know people said this first-time mom thing would be hard, but I didn't believe until now.
Lisa: I remember my first, and I felt completely overwhelmed sometimes. The second has been a little easier.
Kim: Well, I am determined to be the best mom I can be, and I know I can do it. Tom works all day, but he is a lot of help when he gets home.
Lisa: I know how long the day can seem, waiting for help to get there, so don't hesitate to call if you need me.

Dana McAfee

Kim: No, I can do it; I am pretty self-sufficient. My mom struggled when I was little, and I don't want to be like her.

Lisa: I know how strong you are, but some days can be very difficult.

Kim: I am not going to be a failure. I will figure it out, but thank you, really.

Lisa: Kim, don't forget that God has put us here for each other. We are meant to support one another in all things, the weaknesses and the struggles. It isn't a sign of weakness to ask for help it shows you where you need to grow; that's different.

Kim: You know, my mom left us when I was ten. I never got over it. When I got older, I vowed that I would be a better mom. I guess it consumes me sometimes.

Lisa: I can understand that, but you are a different person than your mom and you have Jesus. He will make you stronger and give you wisdom.

Kim: I guess we all can't be the best at everything. I'm sorry. I know I can learn so much from you since you have been through it before.

Lisa: Seriously, I still have to call my mom some days when it all gets the best of me. Don't hesitate.

Love is Not...

Kim: I won't, I promise. Thank you, my friend. What do you say we invade the kitchen and grab a piece of that pie that's left.

Lisa: Perfect fuel for the day! (They exit into the kitchen).

#6
Love is not rude

"...Let today be the day...you speak only the good you know of other people and encourage them to do the same"
—Steve Miraboli, The Life, the Truth, Being Free

It should be one of the easiest things in life to encourage our family and friends, especially when they might not get it anywhere else. However, they can be the last people who get it because we assume they already know how we feel. My heart breaks when I have students in my shows who have no support from family members. It happens more than you think! A parent won't even make the time to see one performance. There can be an excellent crowd and a standing ovation, but if the people they love aren't there, it really doesn't matter.

Rudeness should not be a part of our culture, but it seems to permeate it. Comments, attitudes, and behaviors are filled with it. It is an epidemic. Sometimes we are simply buried in our thoughts, devices, or ignorance. My wonderful niece and nephew know I won't tolerate their phones at the dinner table, and it just takes one look. I don't, however, have control over anyone else. Of course, we all have bad days, or get sad, but we should still make an effort to not involve the world around us in our mess, especially those who live in our personal world and space. We may have no idea how very much a person near us might need a word of encouragement; it might be the one thing that keeps them going that day. One kind word can change a life forever. Paul expressed the impact of Philemon on others, "Your love has given me great joy and encouragement, because you, brother, have refreshed the hearts of the Lord's people." I would love to have the Lord say that to me someday!

I know there are times we just don't think before we speak or we are so preoccupied with something else that we don't notice what's going on around us. We all have what society calls our "resting faces." Mine is not pretty. I can look very angry and feel nothing even close to that, but my face shows it. That is different from letting rude, disrespectful, or harmful words come out of your mouth at any time. James 3:6 has some powerful words, "The tongue also is a fire, a world of evil among the parts of the body. It corrupts the whole body, set's the whole course of one's life on fire, and is itself set on fire by hell." So, basically, if we cannot control our remarks, our language, or our criticism we are committing verbal arson. It can destroy another person.

Love is Not...

Brad – Dad in midthirties
Jason – Son approximately twelve

Brad is sitting at his home desk working on bills. Jason bursts through the door, slams it and heads to his room.

Brad: Woah, hold on! Maybe you could shut the door a little easier the next time. (Jason stands quietly, looking down.) Okay, what's up? Something's wrong. (no response). Come here and sit down. (Jason crosses to a chair and sits) What's going on?

Jason: Why are people so mean? Why can't I have just one normal day without the rude remarks? I hate them!

Brad: Why don't you fill me in on what happened.

Jason: It's just dumb kids who don't understand my love for science. They are always calling me "Science Nerd" or "Astronaut Boy." It makes me so mad! Then, today, Colin joined in. I thought he was my friend?

Brad: That doesn't sound like Colin. I wonder if something is going on with him?

Jason: I don't know and I don't care; they're all jerks!

Brad: Let's think about this for a second. First, you are a very smart boy and that can be a bit intimidating to those who struggle a little more. Sometimes people don't know how to handle that correctly. You know Colin needs extra help in school and that can be embarrassing.

Jason: Why doesn't he just ask me for help, then? We've been friends for a long time.

Brad: Sometimes it is just easier to not face the problem and hide from it. How do you think you should handle this? What have we talked about?

Jason: I know God wants us to be kind to others even when they aren't kind to us, but it's hard.

Brad: Yes, it is. It's even hard as adults. We can disagree with each other and get very bitter about it, but it is always better to handle it with kindness. It also surprises them when I react that way, and they often back down.

Jason: Do you think that would happen with me?

Brad: I can't promise it would be the same, but I know you will eventually feel better about it.

Jason: I'll try, Dad. Thanks for talking to me about it.

Brad: Jason, you can talk to me about anything.

Jason: I know. (stands) I'm gonna work on my homework before dinner. (Jason exits).

#7
Love is not self-seeking

"Almost every sinful action ever committed can be traced back to a selfish motive. It is a trait we hate in other people but justify in ourselves"
– Stephen Kendrick, The Love Dare

It is typical human nature to want to know what we will get out of something, what will benefit us. We get a diploma, we expect a job; we get a new phone, we expect unlimited benefits; we go on a diet, we expect to be a supermodel. These expectations, however, require work. It doesn't just come to us. The people who expect everything to be about them and everything needs to surround them are exhausting! When one of these people is in a relationship, it sucks the life right out of the other person.

Healthy love should be a two-way street. Sharing, working together, common interests, caring about the well-being of the other, and walking side by side through life. Relationships that stand the test of time usually involve the people caring more about the other than themselves. We certainly begin relationships that way. We do everything to win that person's love and affection. So why, when the love is won, do we let our guards down? Any person in our lives should always know how important they are to us, what they truly mean to us. That doesn't mean we have to tell them every day, but we should show them every day, and still tell them often. That isn't easy for those of us who aren't outwardly affectionate people (I am pointing at myself right now). So, we have to find more creative ways to let our loved ones know how important they are. I have a standing dinner most Wednesday nights with a former student and wonderful friend. When I miss those nights, I miss her, so I try to tell her that I missed seeing her. I probably don't have to tell her, but it is important to me that she knows. That is my way. You can find your own way, something unique to your personality, to make another person feel valuable.

Our greatest example of this type of love will always be Jesus. He never thought about Himself when doing the will of his Father, when being ridiculed, when his closest friends deserted Him, when He was hanging on a cross. "God demonstrated his own love for us in this: While we were still sinners, Christ died for us." (Romans 5:8). There is no greater, unconditional, love than that!

Love is Not...

Alicia – twenty-five years old
– It is a week before her wedding, and she is working on final things.

Alicia: (humming a song) I wonder if things will change after the wedding? Eric is so sweet and treats me like a princess. He takes me out, he buys me gifts, he calls me every night. I don't want that to go away. I know we have to build our life together and share responsibilities, but I love the way he makes me feel. I am blessed. (starts to work on decorations) This wedding is exactly what I have dreamed about. My favorite colors, flowers, food, friends (pause)...wait a minute. What is in this for Eric? He has had virtually no say, and he hasn't complained once. How can I be so selfish? When we started all of this planning, I was determined to not be one of those brides, and here I am! I know that most men don't really care about all of the trimmings, but he is still a central person on that day. I need to make sure he knows how important he is in all of this. What can I do for him? How can I make him feel special? I have done a horrible

Dana McAfee

job with this. I need to think of some things I can do for him, starting right now. (takes out phone and calls) Eric? Let's go to dinner tonight, your favorite place, my treat…because you deserve it. See you in an hour. Love you! (walks out to get ready).

#8
Love is not easily angered

"The longer I live, the more I observe that carrying around anger is the most debilitating to the person who bears it"
– Katharine Graham

Our lives seem to be so full of stress these days. Stress breeds frustration, frustration breeds irritation, irritation breeds anxiety, anxiety breeds anger. We don't plan to take it out on those around us, but it always happens. Of course, it would be best to get rid of the stress, but a day at the spa isn't always possible. Learning how to handle the stress would be the solution. According to the people surveyed in 2014 from the American Institute of Stress, there were some strong stress signals:

Physical symptoms caused by stress 77%
Stress increased over the past five years 48%
Annual cost to employers in stress related
    health care . . . .$300 Billion

Dana McAfee

This was a few years ago, Since then we have been through many changes in society, even a pandemic. I can't imagine what stress levels are like now.

When two people are very early on in a relationship, whether friendly or romantic, there is a natural affection that grows. The other person can do no wrong. There are very few arguments and very little anger. As the relationship grows, the guard drops, everyday life settles in, stress creeps in, and irritation begins to grow. The challenge is not to take that anger out on those you love the most. Disagreements will arise, we are human. Those disagreements need to be handled effectively so as not to grow, fester and become cancerous. Once the explosion happens the debris is embedded. We need loving discussions about differences of opinion, opening up new possibilities, listening to each other…laying it all on the table.

I do think a terrible argument in a relationship can cause a great deal of pain, but I also believe there are always opportunities for second chances. Look at Peter's life. Jesus saw his potential and his future, and He continued to pour into Peter's life time and again, in spite of the mistakes and betrayals. Psalm 103:8 says that "God is slow to anger and abounding in love." We have his spirit in us to help us forgive and give second chances where needed. There are many things that justify anger: bullying, mass shootings, the death

Love is Not...

of an innocent, affairs, and many more. Jesus got angry when the money changers were cheating people in the temple. We just need to know how to control the anger, talk about it, and leave the justice up to God. He is always on the side of what is right.

Tammy – Mom – early forties
Stacy – Daughter - eighteen
Mom is sitting reading a book. Stacy walks through the front door.

Tammy: Hi, sweetie! How was your dinner with the girls?
Stacy: It was okay. You know how we are when we get together.
Tammy: You're a little later than you said.
Stacy: Yeah, sorry, we got caught up with everything. (starts to leave the room but comes back) That's not really true, Mom. I didn't go to dinner. I went to a birthday party for one of the seniors.
Tammy: I see. Why did you think you couldn't tell me that?
Stacy: Well, it's not someone I usually hang out with.
Tammy: I don't mind you making new friends.
Stacy: There was drinking, and I knew you wouldn't want me to go.

Dana McAfee

Tammy: You're right.
Stacy: I'm so sorry, Mom. It really wasn't that fun. People are really idiots when they drink. Are you angry?
Tammy: I'm not very happy, but I'm glad you told me. Did you drink?
Stacy: I took one drink, and it was terrible! I don't get the appeal. Please don't be mad.
Tammy: Stacy, you will never do anything to make me not love you. I can be disappointed, and this will not be the last time one of us disappoints the other. I love you beyond bounds. You should know that by now.
Stacy: I do, I really do. No more lies.
Tammy: There will still have to be consequences, and I will talk to your dad about it tomorrow. It will be fair, especially since you owned up to it. Get yourself to bed; we have a busy day tomorrow.
Stacy: Okay. I love you, Mom. Thanks for understanding, See you in the morning.
Tammy: Night. Tomorrow is a new day. Sleep well.

#9
Love keeps no record of wrongs

"Forgiveness is the final form of love"
– Reinhold Niebuhr

When a person is arrested and put on trial, a list of their wrongs is read aloud. Everyone in the courtroom is made aware of all the wrongs that have been done. If the person is found guilty, those wrongs become a part of his permanent record. It will affect what he does for the rest of his life and his sins are remembered, especially by those he has offended. Imagine, if one day in the future, that record is completely erased and the life of the criminal is changed forever. No record of crime left anywhere. That is the power of forgiveness. There is healing, reconciliation, comfort…a new life. Webster defines forgiveness as "to pardon, to cease to feel resentment." The work of forgiveness in a relationship can tear down walls, deepen a bond, renew a friendship, and strengthen love. It is seen in the face of a little child who admits a wrong and is forgiven by a parent, a student who admits to cheating and the teacher gives him a second chance, a spouse who admits feelings of doubt and a desire to make things right and is embraced. The feeling of relief washes over them.

There is nothing that beats down a soul more than someone who continues to remind him of mistakes, errors in judgment, or sin. A child who is told she will never amount to anything because of misguided choices, a teen who is trying to put bad grades behind him but is not given a chance to make things right, a friend who spreads gossip and now wants to tell the truth, but nobody will believe her, a spouse who continues to bring up every instance of wrongdoing, or mistake, that has been committed in a marriage. There needs to be hope for these souls. Forgiveness is that hope. There are numerous places in the Bible that express the importance of forgiveness. One such place is Colossians 3:13: "Bear with each other and forgive one another if any of you has a grievance against someone. Forgive as the Lord forgave you," This type of forgiveness is endless and doesn't appear to be a suggestion. God knows the importance for everyone involved.

The real mystery of forgiveness is that it is really for the benefit of the one who needs to forgive. Bitterness can eat us alive from within. It boils and festers until it creeps into every crevice and there is no room left for love. Forgiveness is the antibiotic that wipes the slate clean and opens the door of the

Love is Not...

heart to love again...feel freedom again. One year we had a convocation at school in our gymnasium. The entire student body (close to 2,000) was there and they walked in a convicted prisoner in his orange jumpsuit. This man had killed a girl while he was driving drunk. He continued to tell the students how his life was destroyed by that one mistake he made and it was very sad listening to the story. But the real impact came when the mother of the girl came up to the microphone and proceeded to tell us all how she had forgiven him and even developed a friendship with him. You could hear a pin drop. Together they go to schools and share their stories so others can learn and, hopefully, not make the same mistake. This is the power of healing and forgiveness.

Courtney & Brandy – Midtwenties
Two friends who haven't seen each other in years. Courtney is sitting on a park bench reading. Brandy walks by, pauses, and turns back.

Brandy: Courtney Stevens? Is that you?
Courtney: Brandy? Hi. It's been ages since I've seen you.
Brandy: (sits) Yeah, I think senior year in high school. Wow, you look great!

Dana McAfee

Courtney: You too. What are you doing now?

Brandy: I just finished my nursing program and looking for a job. How about you?

Courtney: Graduated last year. Just started at an accounting firm a couple of months ago.

Brandy: You were always good at math, and I always struggled. I think we had about every class together that year. I'm surprised we lost touch.

Courtney: I'm not. You really don't remember? I was awful to you that last semester. I was so immature, and I fell in with the wrong group of girls. I thought I made your life miserable.

Brandy: It wasn't pleasant, but it really wasn't that bad. I look back on it and so many of us were struggling with something. Didn't your parents get a divorce?

Courtney: Yeah, it was rough for a while. I didn't handle it well. I guess I took it out on you. I didn't really know how to handle it all. I'm so sorry.

Brandy: Honestly, I never even really thought about it after high school. It makes no sense to dwell on the negative. I had just lost my grandma and we were really close. All I could think about were the things I never got to say to her. She knew how much I loved her, but it made me more aware of having

Love is Not...

              no regrets. I didn't want bitterness to be a part of my life.

Courtney: I wish I could forget. You were always so nice to me and seemed to have it together. I really missed out on a great friendship.

Brandy: What's in the past can stay there as far as I'm concerned. Why don't we meet for coffee next week and catch up? No need to miss out on anything.

Courtney: And start over?

Brandy: Sounds perfect. Here's my number. (puts it in her phone) Next move is yours. (stands) I hope to see you next week.

Courtney: You will!

Brandy exits

#10
Love does not delight in evil

"When I despair, I remember that all throughout history the way of truth and love have always won. There have been tyrants and murderers and, for a time, they can seem invincible, but in the end, they always fall. Think of it always."
– Mahatma Gandhi

Let's be honest. There is something strange about our human nature that makes us gather around an accident, chuckle when someone slips and falls, and feel very satisfied when the person who has hurt us gets what's coming to him. Maybe we don't want to feel like the only person who makes mistakes or gets hurt. This shouldn't be the case, however. When someone we love has a rough time, or finds themselves in a situation that causes pain, we should want to help them out of it and help them find the very best for them. There is enough evil in the world to make its mark; we don't need to add to it. Instead, we should try to look to the good and provide a safe place to run. "Do not be overcome by evil, but overcome evil with good. (Romans 12:21)

Dana McAfee

Early on, in any relationship, we make every effort to encourage, look for the best, laugh and cry together, and generally gush all over the other person. We want to see the best in him and we want him to see the brightest part of us. It seems pretty easy, at the start. As the relationship grows, mistakes are made, selfishness creeps in, schedules get crazy and stress builds. This is when our loved ones need us the most and also when we can fail most miserably.

There are common areas that can develop which cause a level of competition: Who makes more money? Who is a better parent, lover, friend? Who has the most difficult past? Who is more talented? Who is more understanding? If we truly want to show love, we should rejoice when we see these traits in the people we care about and love. Look at it all from a different viewpoint—if he makes more money, you can live in pleasant surroundings; if he is a better parent; you can learn and find balance in the responsibilities, if a better lover, then you benefit; if she has a rough past, then you can minister to her; if she is a better friend, then you are never alone; if he is more talented, then you have a constant source of entertainment; if she is more understanding, then you are less likely to need a psychiatrist! When we want good things for our loved ones, then we can have a wonderful time going through life with them!

Love is Not...

Brandon – Early forties
Just lost a promotion. Comes through the door, pacing

Brandon: I cannot believe he got that promotion over me! I have been there four years longer and work like crazy. He is just a brownnoser and workaholic. It would serve him right if his wife left him for never being home and caring about work more than her. In a couple of years, he's probably going to burn out and get fired, and they better not run to me to fill the position. It's now or never! (sits in a chair and sees his Bible on the table. Picks it up, opens it, and reads.) "So you too should be glad and rejoice with me." What am I saying? I'm just angry and disappointed. I would have liked that raise, but I have everything I need. God always provides, and my family is happy. I know he really needed the raise too, with a new baby on the way. He is very good at his job and a reliable worker, when I go to work on Monday I am going to do my best work and even congratulate him on the new position. I am responsible for what I am given and so is he. Forgive me, Lord, and show me the best way to handle this. Thank you for all you provide and help me never to forget it.

#11
Love does not encourage lies/gossip

"A lie has speed, but truth has endurance"
– Edgar J. Mohn

One activity I used to do with my classes is called The Gossip Game. I whisper a fairly brief message to the first student and each one whispers the message to the next until it is all the way around the room. The final student says the message out loud and everyone looks at each other in disbelief. The message is never the same and very rarely even close to the original. It is an illustration of how gossip can spread through the school and become more and more warped as it progresses. The final product could become intensely damaging for the people involved and is often a lie from the start. Gossip magazines overflow in the racks at the supermarket. Tabloid journalism is rising in the ranks of entertainment shows. When someone starts a juicy story, we love to hear the details, even if it is disguised as a prayer request. Keeping a secret is a myth for many people. We pry them out of those closest to us and "swear" we will never tell another living soul, which lasts until we see our best friend and make her swear not to tell another living soul. We are then surprised when the original source is angry with us when the message gets back to her... and it always does. Now all of the relationships have tension, apologies are given, and we try to go on as before... but it is never the same deep down. That little bit of trust is broken. "A gossip betrays a confidence, but a trustworthy person keeps a secret." (Proverbs 11:13)

We also learn, at a very young age, how to fib. It isn't a lie, of course, just a fib. We become professionals as we get older and learn to lie to others and ourselves for protection. There are even games where you tell three things about yourself and one has to be a lie and the others try to guess which one. A game is one thing, but destroying a relationship is the other end of the spectrum. We need to get back to truth as par for the course. If truth will set us free, then we need to offer up the chains to be loosed. There are times when the truth hurts and those are the times when it needs to be delivered by a loved one, with gentleness, wanting what is best for the other person. Don't confuse truth with an opinion, or someone is jealous and needs to vent. Use good judgment, combined with love, and tell the truth.

Love is Not...

Abby – Late twenties
Heidi – Early thirties
Marion – Early fifties

All are meeting at a coffee shop for a Bible study. Heidi and Marion are at a table. Abby walks in.

Abby: I'm so sorry I'm late, a train again. Always somewhere in this town.

Marion: It's fine, we just got our orders and sat down. Did you want something?

Abby: No, I'm fine for now.

Heidi: I don't know about you, but this book we are reading is really getting to me. Very practical.

Abby: And convicting.

Marion: There are many great principles to learn. Before we dig in, let's take prayer requests and pray. Always a good way to start.

Heidi: James is getting over the flu. It's difficult with him being so young.

Marion: First on the list. Anything else?

Abby: I have two job interviews next week. Need wisdom and courage.

Dana McAfee

Heidi: Oh, I have one, guess what? I just heard that Brenda might be cheating on Greg. It would be awful for his family if they divorce.

Abby: Seriously? I would have never guessed that! They seem so happy. The kids would be devastated.

Heidi: Caitlin is so young too.

Marion: Ladies, we need to pause for a minute. I'm sure you are very concerned about all of this, but did you say you just heard it? From whom?

Heidi: Karen told me at dinner last night. She was with a group of girls—

Marion: Then we need to stop. Did you hear anything from the source?

Heidi: Well, no, but these are really reliable girls.

Abby: I think Marion is right. If we don't know the facts, then we shouldn't be spreading rumors.

Heidi: I was going to have us pray for them.

Marion: Prayer is an amazing thing, and always encouraged, but is it a legitimate request or just gossip at the moment?

Heidi: I see what you mean. I'm so sorry. Greg needs to come to me and ask for prayer.

Abby: A false rumor like that could destroy a family.

Love is Not...

Marion: I know you girls and your hearts are huge. We just need to be careful about adding fuel to a fire we know nothing about. Let's move on for now.

Abby: I'll go order my coffee, and we can pick up with prayer when I get back.

(leaves to get her order)

#12
Love does not encourage injustice

"Never be afraid to raise your voice for honesty and truth and compassion against injustice and lying as greed. If people all over the world… would do this, it would change the earth."
– William Faulkner

The world is becoming a darker place. We don't want to think about it, but there is an influx of crime, shootings, wars, trafficking, abuse… I could go on. Our hearts should break when we see the injustice and cruelty, but too often we choose to wrap ourselves in a bubble of comfort and complacency. We turn our eyes away from the problems and, in turn, miss opportunities to help. It is a sad fact that so many children who are abused, teens who are neglected, women who are raped are afraid to tell anyone because they are made to feel ashamed or told they are liars. There needs to be more protection for those, and countless other, victims. We can have hope as we read in Psalms 103:6: "The Lord works righteousness and justice for all the oppressed." Whether on earth or in eternity, there will be justice.

There is an opportunity, within your relationships, to create an atmosphere of safety for those you love. A spouse should feel the freedom to tell the other any fear or concern and know they have an immediate advocate, someone who will stand up with them and battle the issue at hand. A child should be able to come to a parent with anything and know the parent will help them search for answers and battle the monsters. A friend should be able to trust another with their innermost feelings and know they can pray together, seek counsel, find an ear to listen or a shoulder to cry on. This is where protection should abound, with these important people in your life.

Of course, there will be situations in life where this protection is not enough, or too late, but God understands and hates injustice. He is the ultimate judge, and these are situations where God takes over and gives us the strength we need and points us in new directions. Directions filled with healing and hope. Directions that can't be known in any other way.

Shelly – Early forties
She is sitting in a chair center stage talking to a group of women. The audience can represent the other women or extras can be on stage.

Love is Not...

Shelly: Welcome to the first meeting of Love Protects. I'm so happy to see each and every one of you here, and I hope this will bless your lives as I know it will bless mine. I wanted to give a little background and explain how this will work. First, and foremost, this is a faith-based meeting. I believe that God's love and grace reaches farther than anything else and can reach into any heart, any circumstance. He understands injustice and will walk us through it. Second, I came from a background of abuse as a child and made some very bad choices as an adult. No one is immune from making bad choices but there is no choice that God cannot heal and forgive. Third, you are the victim. You must never let anyone tell you that you are to blame. We will use the next few weeks to help you believe that. This is a safe place and anything that is said stays here. Please know that God hears, and loves, and cries with us. Tell your stories, ask questions, and pray. Healing will eventually come, with God's help. Let's begin. My name is Shelly and I am a victim of abuse....

#13
Love does not doubt

"How we need another soul to cling to, another body to keep us warm, To rest and trust; to give your soul in confidence: I need this, I need someone to pour myself into."
– *Sylvia Plath*

I believe that trust is one of the strongest components in a relationship of any kind. It can strengthen or destroy. Once trust is lost it is almost impossible to get it all back. The relationship will never be the same. There will always be that small voice asking, "Will he do this again? Is she really telling the truth?" It is interesting how so many corporate retreats, counseling sessions, even theater classes, use a trust exercise: fall back and have someone catch you, blindfold someone and lead them through an obstacle course, create a circle and have everyone simultaneously sit in each other's laps. This is because businesses want to trust that their employees will do the right things; healing relationships takes a strong element of give and take; being in a play requires that the actors can cover for each other. Any element of doubt in these situations will weaken the core. If there is any element of doubt that causes hesitation, things can go wrong and people can get hurt. Continued doubt can ruin a relationship. If we continue to doubt the actions or words of those around us then they will stop sharing with us and pull away. No relationship can survive that.

I don't believe that doubt itself is sin. I know God is big enough to handle our questions, and if we dig into scripture when we feel doubts, then it actually helps us grow closer to the Lord as we find answers and learn more about his character. In Jude 1:22 it says to "be merciful to those who doubt." However, if we let the doubt draw us away from Him and His word, then the anger and fear will continue to grow. We can lose our faith and our hope and that is not where we want to be. There are so many things in the world of faith that we don't understand, but that is the definition of faith, "it is the confidence in what we hope for and the assurance about what we do not see." (Hebrews 11:1) God is the only one who knows the future, and we can trust that He will bring us where we need to be, in spite of our occasional doubts.

Celeste – Late thirties
Dale – Early forties

Celeste sits on the couch as Dale enters the living room, late again.

Love is Not...

Dale: Whew, what a day! I didn't think the calls were ever going to end. I guess I should be happy that business is booming. Sorry I missed dinner; I'll just warm something up. It will be as good as always. (pause) You okay? Did you have a rough day? I know your work can get crazy too.

Celeste: It was fine, pretty normal.

Dale: I'm cranking up some good overtime, though. We might be able to start the kitchen in a couple of months.

Celeste: Okay.

Dale: (sits next to her) Now I know something's wrong; what's up?

Celeste: Do you realize how often you have been late this month? Seriously? Work?

Dale: I told you how busy we have been.

Celeste: I called you today to see if we could go to lunch. You weren't there.

Dale: We had a business lunch; I thought I told you.

Celeste: You didn't.

Dale: I guess I just—wait a minute. What are you thinking?

Celeste: What would any wife think?

Dana McAfee

Dale: Celeste, why would I lie? Oh no, you couldn't think? How could you?

Celeste: I don't know, but I have been feeling very lonely lately and frustrated, and you haven't been here.

Dale: Why didn't you say something? I don't have to work the extra hours. I just thought you were in a hurry to start the remodeling. Listen, I will cut back. Starting now. I got so caught up in the work that I didn't notice how it was affecting you. Please forgive me.

Celeste: (tears) I'm so sorry. I shouldn't act this way. You have never given me any reason to doubt you before. I sometimes feel so inadequate, and I miss you. You need to forgive me.

Dale: There is nothing to forgive. I just wish you would have said something sooner. Listen, tomorrow I will come home straight from work, and we can go to dinner. What do you think?

Celeste: I would really love that. We can start on the kitchen any time. I'm in no hurry. C'mon, I will warm up some dinner for you and we can plan our date night.

Love is Not...

Dale: Absolutely. It will be good to spend some time with my best girl.

> (they exit)

#14
Love is not pessimistic

"I suspect the more we can hope for, and it's no small hope, is that we never give up, we never stop giving ourselves permission to try to love and receive love."
Elizabeth Strout – Abide with Me

I have to admit, my favorite Winne-the-Pooh character is Eeyore. In the midst of a downcast spirit, negative outlook, and monotone delivery, I just want to give him a big hug (which I got to do at Disney World one time). His friends rally around him, find ways to encourage him, and sometimes trick him into realizing the positive points in life. They don't give up on him; they want him to be a part of their lives; they try to give him hope... they love him.

According to the Depression and Bipolar Support Alliance, 17.3 million people live with depression in our country every year. A feeling of hopelessness, exhaustion, fear, anxiety, and they struggle to see a way out. They see counselors, they take medication, and rely on the strength of their families. Some can function much better with these treatments,

Dana McAfee

but some don't. There are many negative things going on around us in our world today. Things that make us stop and wonder "Why bother?' "What's the use of trying?" "Why bring a child into this world?" "How will I survive retirement?" Many of us need to start looking for those things that give us hope. Love should be one of those things.

Hope is what keeps us going every day. If we didn't have hope for the future, there would be very little reason to keep going. If we didn't have hope in a relationship, we would never make the first contact. We hope that we will have something in common; we hope there will be a strong connection; we hope that love will grow to last a lifetime. Hope is what drives it all. As soon as that hope starts to die, the relationship starts to fizzle. Maybe we have our hope in the wrong place. When we place our hope in things that can disappoint us, hurt us, or abandon us, then we set ourselves up to experience the worst. Health fails, jobs are lost, mistakes are made, people are not perfect. Our expectations become disappointments. Why not place our hope in the One who will never fail us? The One who understands loss, rejection, and pain. Jesus is our only true hope. When we put our hope in the Lord, we rise up on wings like eagles. (Isaiah 40:31)

Love is Not...

Michelle – late teens
She is in her room packing

Michelle: I can't believe we're moving again! I was just making friends and I really love our church. We're going so far away. I might as well not even try to make friends since I have no idea how long I will be there. I knew we would have to move around with Dad's job; I just didn't think it would be so hard. I am going to keep myself completely closed off in this new place; it's easier that way. I don't want to get too close to anyone. (sees a photograph) Oh, gosh, look at this picture. I really love my youth group. I can't imagine finding friends like this anywhere else, (sits on bed). What's to say I won't? God's love is the same everywhere, and I could easily meet some nice, caring, fun, friendly people. I need to be positive and reach out to others when I get there. Sometimes I would rather stay locked up in my house, but it would get pretty lonely that way. Keeping to myself wouldn't send a positive impression to anyone. If I try not to get close to anyone, I might miss out on some incredible memories. I can still keep in touch with my

Dana McAfee

friends here; that's the wonder of social media (continues packing). I will let God do his work and it will be okay. His people are everywhere I simply need to be open to meeting them. It will be a new adventure, like all the rest.

Mom's voice is heard offstage:

Michelle, dinner's ready.

Michelle: Coming, Mom.

(puts the picture in her suitcase and exits)

#15
Love does not give up

"You may have to fight a battle more than once to win it."
– Margaret Thatcher

How many times can we possibly get our hearts broken and still be open to love in the future? Is there a magic number? Is there an element of severity that makes a difference? A breakup compared to a divorce? A friend moving away compared to a friend betraying you? The heart is broken in all of these circumstances. I have been hurt at times in the past to where I feel like my heart was shattered. A strange thing happened, though. I moved on. I slowly started to heal, find strength, and love again. It might be a different kind of love or a different depth of love, but it is love nonetheless.

It seems that every time I have been broken in my life God gives me a unique opportunity to move in a new direction. That direction might allow me to minister to someone going through a similar circumstance; it might be a new mindset that makes me stronger; or it could be for me to learn to put Him first and not trust in the things of this world. It has

Dana McAfee

never caused me to hate. I've been angry, hurt, confused, depressed... but never hateful. I have felt like giving up, at times, and knew I would never let anyone love me again, but God always had other plans. I am a stubborn person. Independent, to a fault at times. I don't feel like I really need anyone. I guess it depends on the definition of need. One can physically survive without love, but there is an emptiness that can overwhelm a person living like that. We are made in God's image. God is love. We must need it in some aspect in order to understand Him better and those around us.

I am extremely glad that Jesus didn't give up on love when lies were spread about him, his friends betrayed him and ran, he was beaten all the way to the cross, and was killed. Perseverance was shown in every aspect of his life and his words, "Father forgive them, for they know not what they do."(Luke 23:34) "...for the joy set before him he endured the cross, scorning its shame, and sat down at the right hand of the throne of God." (Hebrews 12:2) If he can love through all of that, then I can certainly love through my circumstances. I am convinced if God's love didn't persevere, then this world wouldn't exist. The anger and hate people have toward Him grows every day yet He continues to give all people a chance to know Him. He never gives up on us, and we can learn from that example.

Love is Not...

Rebecca – seventeen
Katie – fifteen
Katie is sitting on a bench outside a classroom. Rebecca is coming down the hall, sees Katie, and stops

Rebecca: Hi, Katie, remember me? I'm in your 2nd period class. I haven't seen you for a few days. You're new, aren't you? (no response) I'm Rebecca.

Katie: Will you just go away and leave me alone!

Rebecca: You really don't look like you need to be alone. You look like you need someone to listen. I'm someone.

Katie: You don't know me at all. You have no idea what I need.

Rebecca: I'm not a mind reader, but I can read people pretty well. I don't like to see people hurting. (sits next to her) I'm not saying I have all the answers, but I can listen.

Katie: What's in it for you? Everyone has an angle.

Rebecca: No angle. You don't even need to talk if you don't want to. I can just sit here for a bit.

Katie: You're a strange one. Most people want something. Some people want a lot.

Dana McAfee

Rebecca: I know, that makes me sad. It costs nothing to be a friend; I wish people knew that.

Katie: You want to be my friend?

Rebecca: Of course! We can't have too many friends in our lives.

Katie: You're different, you seem nice. I'm not used to that. You also don't know when to quit, do you?

Rebecca: (smiles) Not when I think something is worth it. If you want, we could meet after school and set up a time to get pizza. I could introduce you to some of my friends; they would really like you.

Katie: I have to catch the bus, but I will try to be there. Thanks, Rebecca, I haven't met many nice people.

Rebecca: Well, we are going to change that. (stands) See you by the buses after school. (exits)

#16
Love never fails

"There is no failure except in no longer trying"
– Elbert Hubbard

There are many things in this life that I am not good at and I can acknowledge those things without destroying my self-confidence. I will never sing on Broadway; I will never understand modern technology; I don't know how my car works; I can't do math without a calculator; and I am not good with small children, which is why I teach high school. I don't think of myself as a failure because of these things, instead I try to find the things I am good at and enhance those skills. God has given us all different skills so we can be there for each other.

When it comes to relationships, I'm not really sure where I fall in the spectrum. I'm a good listener, I enjoy being around people, I am usually patient, and it really isn't difficult for me to forgive. Even though I think I am pretty good at these things, I don't think I get it right 100 percent of the time. I don't have it in me to be perfect, none of us do. However, God does. One of my favorite verses is Romans 8:38

- 39; "For I am convinced that neither death nor life, neither angels nor demons, neither the present nor the future, nor any powers, neither height nor depth, nor anything else in all creation, will be able to separate us from the love of God that is in Christ Jesus our Lord." If we want to get any relationship principles right, then we have to rely on the only one who gets it right 100 percent of the time. He will never fail. I am encouraged with this fact. If I want to continuously love, then I have to let Him love through me. This promises a much higher rate of success.

Love comes in so many forms and we can start small: a hug or smile, a listening ear, a meal for a struggling family, an encouraging note or text, sitting with someone in a hospital room, cooking dinner, or doing dishes for your spouse, attending your child's play... game... concert, standing up for someone who can't stand up for himself. The list goes on and, with God's help, never fails. Love makes a difference in all of our lives.

Peter
Has just talked to Jesus after the resurrection

Peter: I can't believe what I just heard! How can He still want to use me? I've failed in so many ways. I open

Love is Not...

my mouth, and I have no control over what comes out. I make promises, I break them. I want to have this incredible faith and I doubt. How can He forgive me after I betrayed him? How can He still love me? I am so ashamed and yet He doesn't make me feel that way. After all of my mistakes, He wants me to build his church, take care of His people, and share the good news. I will make it my life's mission! I will rely on His help to reach out to others and tell of His great love. Only a love like this could forgive me, love me. Everyone needs to know this unchanging, sacrificial, unending love. I am the example; I will proclaim it forever. I will start right now where I live and see where it takes me. Thanks be to God!

(he rushes off).